PEA SOUP

PEA SOUP

New & Selected Poems

CHRIS BASHER

Printed in the United States of America

First Printing

ISBN: 9798327982710

Published by *Kindle Direct Publishing*
Seattle, Washington 98109

Cover Photo by *iStock by Getty Images*
Cover Design by *Amazon-Kindle*

The publication of this book is made possible by the Heavenly Council on the Arts.

Author contact: pdklinebooks@gmail.com
Website: https://www.pdklinebooks.com

CONTENTS

ACKNOWLEDGEMENT

It is hard to argue that Ted Kooser is not one of our greatest contemporary American poets. Having won the Pulitzer Prize and earned the title of U. S. Poet Laureate by themselves would negate any such argument. Thousands of poems, numerous and successfully published volumes, and consistently high praise from respected sources provide further confirmation.

"We had known, some of us, that Ted Kooser was good. He has with his wit and his earthiness, his imagination and his lucidity, staked out as his own a region – western it is – somewhere poetically between Frost and Williams (he shows us, to our surprise, how close they were)."

—Theodore Weiss

"Ted Kooser must be the most accessible and enjoyable major poet in America. His lines are so clear and simple."

—Michael Dirda, *The Washington Post*

"That Kooser often sees things we do not would be delight enough, but more amazing is exactly what he sees. Nothing escapes him; everything is illuminated."

—*Library Journal*

You will not get any argument from me, one who taught American Literature to high school Honors English students and others; who wrote, read, and studied poetry most of his life. I received all the confirmation I needed when Ted Kooser replaced Robert Frost at the top of my favorite-poets list. That sounds frivolous, of course. The significance rests with me alone, for only I know how much and for how long I have revered the poetry of Robert Frost, not to mention others who are high on my list – Dickinson, Whitman, Williams, Hughes, Stevens, cummings…

And yet, none of that explains the reason I am dedicating this book to Ted Kooser and here acknowledging his contribution to this volume. That he would recoil at the mere mention of comparing poets or writing poetry for the sake of popularity is a big part of the reason. In his own words:

"Any well-made poem is worth a whole lot more to the world than the person who wrote it."

"The essence of being a poet is in the writing, not in the publications or the prizes."

Mr. Kooser's poetry, as with his character, exudes humility – humility in an earthen sense. As in taking off your coat and tie and rolling up your pantlegs and sleeves to romp in vast fields of words, language, images, and feelings; as in removing shoes and socks and feeling the rich soil work its way between the toes. The air is cool, clear, and pure, and nowhere else do you feel as free, free to take as much time as you want to find the perfect words to go with the perfect language, together that fit with the perfect image and feeling so that meaning and truth light up like fireflies.

I have enjoyed feeling so alive in that way that I did not notice when I wandered into parts of fields where readers rarely go without getting lost, where they never do see the fireflies. They get lost only because they do not need or want to take the time to find and follow my tracks, no matter how carefully I have stepped.

Therein lies the greater part of Ted Kooser's contribution to this book. He helped me find even greater joy by watching where I'm going and not wandering too far from where readers park their cars, spread their blankets, and roll out their coolers. Only then did I stop being a poet long enough to savor special moments and some refreshment in the company of those with whom I long to connect.

Ted once questioned why I was using a pen name (P. D. Kline). It took a while for me to realize why that mattered to him. Although it was the name given to me at birth and changed at the time of my adoption, all of which had meaning for me, how would my readers know and why would they care? What would it have to do with the poems I write? In other words, in Michael Dirda's terminology, I could be more "accessible."

I proudly join many others in gratitude for Ted Kooser's contribution to American literature and the enjoyment of reading poetry.

For Ted Kooser

1

"Poetry is when an emotion has found its thought and the thought has found its words."

—Robert Frost

EMBERS

There was a wood-burning stove in the kitchen,
the one my cherished aunt used for more than fifty years
for cooking food and thawing mittens. She'd let me fill
the fire box under the heavy metal plates where pots

would boil and frying pans sizzle – a simple stove,
cast iron strong. It'd warm the house – first floor
and most of the second. Talk about lasting value,
I couldn't see how it'd ever break down –

nothing to plug in or hook up, no wires, gauges, gas lines,
or built-in electric clock. A gaumy egg-timer, mason jar
half-filled with wooden matches, and wind-up clock sat
in the center of a chrome and Formica table

flanked by matching chrome and vinyl chairs –
three that matched, duct-taped and old as the stove.
No way that stove could fit through any door in the house
(Back then, I thought it was there before the place was built).

Still, it was the only home I knew that had one
for cooking, a perplexing semblance of our family's
privation. Even we had a used electric range,
stained as it was with a bad element.

Funny how the things she cooked smelled so good
and tasted even better, how stoves and people go
away, but their value stays behind, rekindling
and radiating warmth, like when I stoked the embers.

AN EIGHT-YEAR-OLD'S RIDE TO GLORY

Over miles of open land, he lost himself
in the rhythm of his horse's heavy hooves
pounding the prairie turf. The breeze
they made felt cool upon his face,
his Stetson slapping at his back.

Most of all, he loved the leather saddle
that felt and smelled the way he knew
it would, his feet snug in the stirrups,
his Wrangler jeans as tough as Lucas McCain,
and a bark-less wooden six-gun in his belt.

When it was time to rest his trusty steed,
he climbed down from the tree happy with
the time he'd made and looking up ahead
for Paladin, who was waiting there for him
with Rafter, his brave and loyal thoroughbred.

They tip-toed to the top of the ridge,
the deep but crusty snow holding the weight
of his steps. The ice-crunching sound cracked
the still of the winter chill, like the clink and
clatter of his menacing, silver-plated spurs.

PERFECTION

Turning its head far beyond what
he could ever do, a robin
hopped in silent bursts, listening
for worms. A sun-bright yellow finch
clung to a thistle sack, looking
all around. A rabbit nibbled
at the clover, looking around
and darting beneath the neighbor's
lilac bush. On a nearby roof peak,
a mockingbird was looking all
around, learning, watching Passion's
messenger streaking fire and grace
all the way to its chosen branch,
and the man who sat in silence,
looking all around, sensing change,
feeling part of its perfection.

WHAT MATTERS

The water fought for space,
frozen family fragments
bursting, landing different
places, until he left
with less than fifty years,
gone before gathering
the pieces, telling them
what matters. In the end

he did. Quickly did the
fragments melt in tears from
hearts in flames, cascading
back together, pooling
on the floor. The discord
binding understanding
limped away, thorny tail
between its fiendish legs.

IN THE TREES BY A LAKE

In this shot, she sits upon the cabin steps
in pigtails, a chipmunk at her side, her new
best friend nibbling on a piece
of peanut-butter bread forty years ago.

In this one, she sits upon the condo steps,
pigtails gone, a chipmunk tiptoeing toward
a nearby peanut-butter pretzel treat.
More pixels, greater clarity.

So many years have passed, or have they?
Our faces, places, circumstances changed,
yet still I see the pigtails in her eyes
and keep a jar of Peter Pan nearby.

LOCKED INSIDE

In his daughter's eyes, there came
to be a calmness, not the eye
of passing hurricanes, her voice
no longer gale-force gusts that thrashed
against the door, more like bamboo
wind chimes swaying on the porch
with peaceful spirits passing through.
In wind and freezing rain, hailstones
larger than a family's home,
category five perspectives,
and drifts that piled up against her door,
she couldn't see his hand or hear
his voice. Nearly twenty years it took
for her to reach the door, try the knob,
and see the lock was on the inside.
Unlocked, the knob fell to the floor,
the door swung, and a weather-beaten
father stumbled in, dressed in jubilation.

BULLY

The bully stomped in, loud-mouthed
and tossing cherry bombs at the sky,
their flash unmasking thunderheads,
their blasts landing in our room,
I guess to make us wince and fear
what else he'd do, grumbling the way
he did, spittle spraying from his angry
face, eyes flaring and searching
for someone else to scare.

Beneath the bed, my wimpy
sister hid, but not me. I stood at
the window watching the creep push
his way through trees and yards, spewing
brutish threats – and, just like that,
he left, kicking leaves about and spilling
our next-door neighbor's garbage can.
Little ol' me could've done all that,

so why the fuss? The thing is,
someone only had to hear about
the chance he'd come to close
the schools and hide inside.
(Schools closed – *talk about*
escaping looming danger!) In hasty
thankfulness, without thinking
through the things I'd rather do,
I ran outside to bag our neighbor's trash.

YOU FORGOT TO TURN THE LIGHTS OUT WHEN YOU LEFT

Why did I cry when each of you died?

You let yourself go when you knew to him
        it mattered –
while YOU broke your vows when you knew
        what it would do to her.

You couldn't have your own, and the renamed,
        second-hand child couldn't mean the same.
So, you nagged, chided, railed, and hit him
        with the heel of your shoe –

With that, YOU failed to time the collision
        for her passenger-side seat.
Both of you skidded into the ditch intact, one of the few
        things you did together, that and the divorce.

When that didn't cause the pain for him you hoped,
        you moved us eight states away –
while all YOU would have stopped was the child support
        a judge made you send.

Why did I cry when each of you died
        those many years later?

FLIMFLAM

Last week he stared at trees
looking for a humble,
understanding branch, fit
to hold the weight, and there
they were like arms with hands
that beckoned him.
Ignored were leaves that lay
about their trunks, the leaves
they could not save, rotting
the way they do. Sensing
guile, he tasted hope
in air his lungs absorbed,
rejoicing as they did.

ADIRONDACK SUNSET

The setting sun has calmed the lake
and crowned the mountaintops with gold.
The gold has spilled onto the lake,
and on it flows into my soul,
enlightened, purified – whole.

OLD POET

While shambling from his berth to where
he liked to write, he thought the train
was gaining speed, for from his window
seat a metaphoric blur was all he saw.
Fearlessly, he found the door and jumped
into his lake of memories, dredging
darker depths for what was left.

II

"To see a World in a Grain of Sand, And a Heaven in a Wild Flower."

—William Blake

WESTERN FLYER

He loved the contoured grips, streamers
like blue flames shooting from a jet's engines
when he pedaled into high speed, a perfect fit
for his white-knuckle grip, and he never let go.

Other boys did, hands at their sides
or stretched like wings soaring into space.
He thought they were brave and free,
but reckless to a sin. Not him.

Fast forward fifty years. All that's left is on
its way to the dump – engines past repair,
bent frame, rusted chain, brittle tires cracked
and flat, and grips worn thin to the bone.

TEXTING

She didn't see me wave as she pedaled
past our place and on down the street, one hand
on the handlebar, the other cradling
the phone, her thumb performing "Little Bell"[i]
     across the tiny keyboard.

She didn't look up as Death sped by in
a red Dodge Charger with wide tires and face-
rattling bass. No time to brake had she swerved
into its path. She never would have known
     what hit her.

She didn't see the toddler chasing
a rabbit toward the street, and never
heard the mother shouting, warning her
to stop, nor did she see the baby rabbit
     darting in between her tires.

Cars parked along the street tried diving for
the grass but froze in fear as she brushed by,
the fabric of her life caught in the chain,
her wheels of time flipping, spinning, tumbling
     overhead.

LIGHT OF LIFE

In a nearby Leyland cypress,
a flickering firefly was all
        he had to see
to light his way to memories –

Around the yard she'd chase
and catch them in a jar he'd keep
inside his heart.

On a celestial scale, as in a solar eclipse,
the alignment of their hearts and God's
        was all he needed
to light his way back to life.

DAD

We brought the birthday gift
to your room – official
John Deere logo baseball cap,
six panels with a button on top.

We hoped you'd look forward
to wearing it next time
you romped around the yard
on your John Deere riding mower.

You clutched the brim in gratitude,
or so I thought, the stroke
having plundered your speech
and strapped you to the bed.

Now I hate the thought it may
have been reminding you
of what had come and gone
instead of what was yet to be.

Even worse the nurse, who couldn't
grasp the meaning of the moment,
unhappily stationed next to the bed
to keep the tube down your throat.

We keep the gift on the shelf, unworn,
next to your flag, precisely folded,
blue field visible within its glass case,
which has a way of reflecting

the look on your face that day, a look
transcending physical degradation.
It wasn't fear, resignation or defeat –
more like dignity, love and freedom.

DAWN'S LAKE

On the dock between two wooden rails,
an intricate web of silk was spun through the night
to snag a sleepy skeeter.

On the lake between two mountain sides,
an intricate web of fog was spun through the night
to snag a sleepy skier.

Fresh from its latest victory over night, dawn
exposed the dew-ridden gossamer and winked
as its legions swept in, scattering the fog in every direction.

AGAINST THE WIND

A swallow sits atop the weathervane
looking where the arrow points,
knowing it's the way to go,
but wishing it were with the wind.
Instinctively, it springs to flight
against the surge, over the road,
past the field, and into a dark,
abandoned barn.

An aging man watches, wondering
why that's the way it is.
Having waited too long, he springs
from the fence where he was leaning,
his legs tottering against the surge,
past a fallen tree, a shattered
flowerpot, and into a dark
and empty house.

LIFE AND DEATH

Without intent, I stepped upon a frog,
    its insides out, the stain
upon my patio a Rorschach test
    for me to think about.

Pure chance there was no chance for him beneath
    what for the tiny frog
a monstrous foot belonging to a man
    who stepped before he looked.

In church that day, I watched a bug beneath
    our pew crawling toward
the altar, until that monstrous foot mashed
    it through the Berber threads.

Neither frog nor bug could have understood
    its life and death, or why
a size fifteen would suddenly emerge
    to end its time to be.

The same it is with God and me more than
    the frog and bug combined
and multiplied by all my selfish years,
    which causes me to ask

by what more contribution I have made
    than either life I crushed
a size infinity, golden shoe has not
    yet crushed and splattered me.

That chance would have me make it this far
    allows no peace of mind,
but rather my forgiving God, who looks
    before He steps.

RAILROAD CROSSING

Days like passenger railcars streaked by,
      nearly a blur,
my head turning the speed of each
      to see inside,
to find a face, someone I knew
      and wished to see
before they all had passed.

They seemed to pick up speed, no time
      to catch each one,
faster toward the one I knew
      would come
bound for where it had to go on the
      track where it was placed,
no brakes to hit or switch to kick.

Red lights flashed, steam whistle blared, bells clanged,
and gates locked in place as if to warn us all
of what was passing.

When the lights stopped flashing
      in my mind,
I fixed upon the last car passing
      and getting smaller.
Farther down the tracks, the whistle
      blew again
as if to scream, "Slow down!"

Horns blared, cars and fingers whipped out and around me,
across the track, pedal to the metal, almost
as though there were a train to catch.

JOY'S INTERMENT

I watched the priest walk around their child swinging his terrible
thurible, filling the air with incense as though to chase away
the shade of death, as if joy had not succumbed within
the linen-draped box and hearts of those kneeling near
to what was far, far away.

The heavy scent filled my lungs, as though to storm
the shadow searching me for other joy to kill,
as if the wood from pews had not encased
and sealed my heart in darkness, latched
by words entombed in ritual.

The sound came from high above our heads,
a sky light with stained glass wings of doves,
the thud of a bluebird against the pane
trying to get out, again and again.

HOUSE SPARROWS

A twenty-nine-ninety-five, True Value birdhouse,
solid wood, unvarnished, unpainted, hangs
on the shed not three flaps of your wings away.
For last year's squatters, it was good enough
for raising two or three sets of quintuplets,
from which you may be one. Yet you build new
in our patio umbrella, beneath which we walk,
sit and talk. Not another consumer trend I hope,
or perhaps you're trading country life for the city,
or house hunting for the pure joy of it.

POP-POP'S FINAL BATTLE

He made it through the day, her birthday, like an old,
beleaguered soldier coming out of the trees, but not
unscathed, memorable moments like bullets that
strafed his mind throughout the day and night,
some like sidewinders locked upon his heart –

rocking her to sleep, first words and steps,
running and jumping in leaves, celebrating
footprints in the sand; dancing, singing,
hide and seek, and kindergarten graduation…
Life-giving times, life-taking memories.

Dawn at last arrived with reinforcements –
a rising sun, the morning air, the smell of food…
Out of the woods and into the light, having flung
his guns, he marched toward something new, not far
nor fast enough to stop a stray slug from drawing blood.

III

"One day I will find the right words, and they will be simple."

—Jack Kerouac

TRACK MEET

From what I dragged myself away I don't recall
(It wasn't worth remembering), just that I found
someone I knew with a smattering of parents
halfway up the empty stadium seats. Why there
I wasn't sure, until I turned and saw the view,
a perfect vantage point – Except for end zone
bleachers, I could see the whole track that circled
the hallowed high school football field.

No sooner did I sit than a pistol's loud clap
unleashed the pack in a wave of adrenaline
that engulfed us where we watched.
Four hundred forty yards away, a victory each boy
longed to wear at school, their parents'
anxious hearts pushing at their backs.

It wasn't hard to find him, for he broke away
in the wrong direction, dead last, my excitement
skidding on the cinder. "Wait," my friend advised,
seemingly speaking from experience (an odd
response for such a hopeless circumstance).
They entered the first turn that wound behind
the bleachers, a silhouette of runners,
his rivals spreading out ahead of him.

Down the backstretch the pace quickened,
but he wasn't losing ground. In fact, no longer
was he last. By itself that seemed like something

to applaud, if only he would persevere and not fall
any farther back. The thing is, he held his stride;
it was the next boy who slacked and fell behind.

Entering the far turn, it seemed that others may
be losing stride, for onward through the turn
he took the lead – somehow the *lead*.
The nearest boy, who thought the race was his,
launched a gallant dash, and yet the gap increased.
There, soaring down the homestretch with wind
beneath his wings, a better part of me, the limits
of my perspective blown away in gusts of wonder.

HEADING SOUTH

A chilly autumn wind blew into town from the north
on its way through Delaware behind the blue winged teal,
who welcomed the lift, no doubt the topic of discussion
on Salt Pond where they stopped to bathe, feed, and rest,
until the sudden plunk and splash of a golf ball
and the cursing of a stomping, looming species
out ahead of his wobbling, cackling coterie.

That northerly wind was howling with joy. Like a Yankee
center fielder, it had snagged his Pro V-1 on the dead run,
dropping it to its double-bogey death. The man kept coming
in a fit of rage, flinging his wedge into the middle of the pond.
Only then did the dabbling ducks resume their flight,
looking back beneath their wings to see one of his straggle
with a quiver full of shiny reeds running to keep up.

POSTCARD MORNING

Early this morning I opened the backdoor
and stepped out into a postcard with Bailey,
our dog. Based on the forecast yesterday and
the trucks out treating roads, snowfall overnight
was expected, but not the white, buttercream
frosting on every branch, roof, patio chair
and figurine. The baker must have worked through
the night, for every link in the chain link fence
was white, just like the weathervane on top of
the shed, which didn't dare budge for fear
of disturbing its masterful makeover.

The dog and I were the only things moving,
the only sound this Saturday morning, as though
everyone had left, until a sparrow emerged
from its apartment in our neighbor's hedge,
looked around, quivered, and went back inside.

After checking the premises by sight and sniff,
Bailey went about his business dutifully, without
a thought of yesterday's snowless drab.
Meanwhile, I tried to find the edge to flip
and address this perfect postcard. Selecting one
with whom to share my joy distracted me until
I realized how I could send the card to everyone.

REPLACEMENT

Some days our Lab fills the void,
taunting me with my hat or slipper
until I leave the kitchen of my thoughts
and pay attention – like playing tug,
or taking him out to sniff his way around
the nearby field, or holding the bone
he brings me for a gift, or letting him pull
my laces loose, or scratching his back
and rubbing his feet, or other almost
lovable rituals.

Other days I can't be fooled and won't
come out to play. I shut the door
and plug my ears when he reminds me
of the ones he can't replace. When
I peek out and see him waiting
all that time outside my door,
I almost want to let him in
for fear I am the void.

SONG IN ARCADIA[11]

Among the Meadow-rue and Turtlehead
    your spirit sings to sooth the Red Admiral,

then leaps into the pan of corn you bring
    to Scratches, Patches, and Precious,

who wait outside your door the way they did
    before they shed their spots.

Along the forest floor it cheers the Juncos'
    foraging for seed and takes its breath

from wings of hummingbirds that dart
    among the Columbine,

then off to host a Fritillary tour of gourmet
    garden tastes you cultivate.

It sweeps along the South Shore Road,
    hands free and arms wide open

where all can hear it sing, from loons
    to Lady Ferns, bears to Luna Moths,

Hobblebush to Painted Ladies, coyote,
    Swallowtails, dragonflies, et al.

Its sustaining song of peace and love
    whispers through the conifers

and sugar maples, and ripples through
    the Fulton Chain of Lakes,

all to the music playing in your husband's
    mind and heart.

THE GIFT

Pulling away from the curb and disappearing
around the corner was the ghost of my biological past.

The old Dodge moved slowly, but with strength
and purpose in apt personification of its driver,

my eighty-nine-year-old grandmother, having driven
fifteen hundred miles after most of my adopted life

had passed till then, to meet my bride and hug
our children for the first time, to see where once

she lived and worked (another northeastern city
dying with its factories), to have me drive

to nearby towns and peek through cracks in rooms
my mind had sealed: lush meadows on a hilly farm

where my father played, the church in which
he carried candlesticks (I touched the holy water

as though to feel his DNA), surviving friends
she hadn't seen in thirty years (their stories

like golden nuggets dropping from the sky
and pelting walls I'd worked so hard to build),

neglected graves of those unknown to me
(brothers gone before they walked, a grandfather).

She told me things I never would have found
in the precious few black and whites sent to me.

Pulling away from the curb and turning the corner
of my life, she had delivered her priceless gift,

which I had just begun to unwrap, its value doubling
every time a part of me broke free and bolted for the corner.

PITA[III]

My patron saint of lost causes,
whom I'd protect, for whom I'd die
("a life for a life"[iv]), snatched away
from those whose love transcends
the world by those whose love has
acquiesced to that which is not love,
to all that is not true.

"Be not overcome by evil, but
overcome evil with good."[v]

My Pita, do not let go of all that's pure
and true, of hope and all that's
right, of God's love I have for you.

BUSINESS ACUMEN

He sat on a leafless branch close to where I parked
on the abandoned boat ramp at Wyoming Lake.
Like a farmer spinning the cob and sinking his teeth
into its soft, butter-slathered kernels, this young,
gray squirrel spun his walnut with dexterity
like a seasoned juggler. He carefully chewed each
morsel, then spun the nut again before taking
another bite. The pattern held until he dropped
the half-eaten nut to the ground and scurried along
a northbound branch. Perhaps he hadn't signed out
or was late for a meet-and-greet. Back on the lake
were Canada geese, arrivals and departures
under proficient air-traffic controls. Having
wolfed a fruit, cheese, and nut salad, washing it down
with a twelve-ounce cappuccino, I checked my watch,
backed to the road, and sped to the office, daring
not to miss my one o'clock annual review.

TOOTH EXTRACTION

"Good-morning, how are you?" a cheerful Dr. Moeller asked.

"Quite well, now that your assistant assured me this is not the first of these you've done."

"She's right. It's my second," quipped the D.D.S., somewhat amused and checking his syringe.

I could tell he wanted to do something with my mouth. "I'm also glad to hear you weren't out partying last night."

"But I was. A few beers to celebrate my first."

"If you have any left, I could use one now!"

I couldn't tell, but he may have chuckled as the needle pierced my gums, extra shots just to be sure.

With fingers, gauze, mirror, probe, and vacuum cleaner nozzle in my mouth, there was no room for a comeback, so I focused on the long, lanky, angular legs, beneath which I was pinned. They barely fit from floor to ceiling – a monstrous daddy long-legs! Its pedipalps were shaved smooth, sanitized, and sparkling – One held a blinding spotlight for my tormentor, another his tray of scrubbed and stainless implements (or were they?), which made me think of the Iron Maiden,[vi] Brazen Bull[vii] and Pear of Anguish.[viii] Still another could have been armed for problem patients – novocaine for the brain, perhaps.

Halting that train of thought was his fait accompli,
the string he tied to the stubborn tooth (or any tooth
would do), and his eager CDA swing-slamming
the chamber door with one hand while stroking
my forehead with the other and telling me
how well I was doing.

Barely conscious through the suturing and certain they
were snickering, I staggered out the office door,
merrily on my way.

BIRTHING SPRING

lingering
brittle falling
leaf,
brilliant colors
faded,
brushing past
a sapling limb,
its node, stem,
root brimming
with sun, water,
wonder of life
blossoming

PEA SOUP

It was then I knew what it'd be like, a sun that wouldn't rise,
a day that'd lose its warmth, dawn that'd sleep in, and fog
that wouldn't care enough to leave.

It was the look in your eyes when you wouldn't look at me,
when you cursed the damnable stroke and whispered
the years you had together. Your voice never faltered,

and there was a chilling loss of warmth in your eyes,
a fog bank that wouldn't lift. Somewhere in that pea soup,
you trudged alone, unable to see where your feet would land.

The violets you loved and nursed on the windowsill were parched.
Your bony hands rested on the kitchen table, wrapped around
the mug of decaf you didn't drink, as though to feel his warmth.

IV

"Poets are damned but they are not blind, they see with the eyes of angels."

—William Carlos Williams

ATLANTIC COAST ART EXTRAVAGANZA

This particular mobile, outdoor art studio and exhibit came
from points north and stopped in Dover, probably heading south
to Norfolk. Each unique "canvas" was large enough to span
a boxcar or tanker, one after another left along New Burton Road
for optimal viewing.

The freestyle nature of the artists' strokes was not lost in their
precision. Shapes and colors saw to that with wild-eyed,
in-your-face expression, more cubistic than abstract.
Broken faces and letters that didn't form words that I could tell,
and yet they seemed to have so much to say –

an aimless life's hopelessness, or the loneliness of one's
obscurity, or longing to bust from zippered body bags of expectations.

Assuming they worked by moonlight to ensure their requisite solitude,
I hoped the studio was parked for the night. It'd be worth foregoing
sleep to watch a member of their special guild come dressed
in shadows with his bag of colors, for there was enough space
to claim his place and add his latest masterpiece.

The loud, jolting slam of the Norfolk Southern's couplings shook
me from my captivation. The studio lurched and crawled along the track,
slowly picking up speed and moving on to its next scheduled showing.
When the last car passed, I saw a young man not yet twenty years
of age, a ragged, paint-stained backpack hanging from his shoulder.

Assuming he was one of them and wanting to hear his thoughts, I started toward the tracks in his direction, but he walked away, picking up speed and disappearing down Webbs Lane. I was going to ask him what it meant to have his work showing in more states and cities than most painters ever dreamed, but he and the Atlantic Coast Art Extravaganza were gone.

EVENING PRIMROSE

Her entrance was grand, precisely planned,
having waited a lifetime for the moment,
her formal gown of finest fabric, visibly soft
and richly hued, no less the color of the sun.

The night had just arrived, and she, dancing with
the setting sun and a rising, jealous moon,
her arms waving with the swaying of her finery,
sent her rivals home to sleep and dream.

This was her time, and she guzzled its nectar,
cavorting through the night in unrelenting
flamboyance, blind to the light of a new day
when her beauty withered within her gown.

The next night, her star-crossed sisters,
seduced by the sun and moon, unpacked
and dressed to keep her quest alive,
to dance on through the night until they died.

DOGGED WISDOM

Of the three new plantings, two Leyland cypress and a blue spruce,
our yellow lab prefers the Leyland near the end of the yard.

The sequence is the same each day – He buries his face in the soft,
fragrant branches, picks up the scent of the rabbit or squirrel

that lounged in the dirt around the tiny trunk, and pees where he stands.
In the best end zone dance I've seen, he claws the ground in mighty
swipes,

front right and back left paws first, the others next in perfect sync,
divots slung into the air behind him, head held high in triumph,

eyes forward, never looking back, content with what he produced
in the moment, no thought of yesterday or what may come tomorrow.

The older I get, the more I realize how much I'd love to pee like that.

ADK DIAMONDS

As the earth turns just right,
the diamonds rise for all
who have eyes to see.
It is their time to reflect
their priceless treasure trove,
wary of clouds prowling over
Black Bear Mountain.
See the gems withdraw
to their perfect hideaway
from where they watch
the rippling pellets of rain
and wait upon the sun's return.

FEEDER

He pulled the curtain back from where
he sat waiting for sleep, as though
it would wander through the window
screen to take his hand. Close by on
the other side of the screen hung
the feeder, lifeless yet alive,

like the forbidden pub he passed
each foggy, predawn hour with his
bag of papers, rolled and dated
six decades ago. He was surprised
the scent of them had followed through
the years to join him there, that night.

He wondered where his banqueters
slept, what their lives were really like,
what their options were. Forced to
retire, he worried that it'd hang
there empty and desolate when he
couldn't buy the thistle seed.

The night crept in and huddled in
the corner with the paperboy
and senior VP, knowing it too
would soon be a memory.
He tried to ignore them and the
others who were pushing their way in

by watching the feeder, imagining birds
clothed in regal colors, full of life
and stopping in on their way to where
they're going, unconcerned about
the seed they know they'll find,
and never looking back.

SNAPSHOT

When I removed
the training wheels,
he found another freedom,
bike pitching to the side
of his next exhilarating
thrust upon the pedals.
A new kind of wind in
his face swept through
his hair and fed his heart
with joy, all preserved
in a Kodak flash
that dashed past years
of undeveloped moments.

AS IF TO BOIL A FROG

Except on days it rained, he walked the yard,
obsessively eradicating every flaw,
a mini field of green without a variant shade.

He watched the infiltrator, a single creeping
bindweed petal, rich in color, soft in touch,
to which he granted merciful stays of execution.

Next time he mowed was soon enough,
but then he mowed around it's blossoms,
three more swimming in his lake of virgin green

and heading for the porch. Their brash objective
he dismissed, convinced that there was always
time to pull the roots and save the lawn.

or leave their subterfuge to flower-killing frost.
A month would pass from autumn's chill before
he thought to check again and extirpate

the wicked weed. Its beguiling petals somehow
survived and still he let it go, convinced
that neighbors scoffed at his obsession.

In wintry lassitude, he did not want to see
the course his hijacked glory took, somehow
through the cracks in his foundation,

beneath the rug, up through his favorite chair, and on into his brain. By summer he was pulling grass that hadn't drowned in his sea of weeds.

A MAN

The chair's length and width,
with size-fifteen Croc wedged
in the footrest, say he is a large man.
The dates and times of journal entries
left upon a nearby stand say that's where
he sleeps and writes in early morning hours.
The glasses, blanket, pen, and lamp agree.
The unused bed and chest of drawers suggest
a guestroom commandeered for something else.
Precisely hung, seemingly by age, a family shrine
of white-framed portraits intimates a man
of many years, and one of love and sorrows.
Shelves high and long of poetry, biography
and history say he is a thinking man who's
searching, learning, validating. The empty
closet says he's gone. The room intact
the way he left it says he's loved
perhaps more than he knew.

MERRY CHRISTMAS

The sky a perfect blue,
no cloud in view. Grass
so green no weed is seen,
despite the time of year.
Our faded siding freshly
painted, or so it seems.
The dog's bark not so
loud and jarring to
the nerves. The room
where I sit alone
and write more like
a children's playroom
than an aging man's tomb.
More often am I walking
to give myself a chance
of seeing yellow finches
back upon their favored
branch. What's left
of flowers in your Nana's
pots seeming to burst in life
anew. How blessed be days
not left imagining all of us
together with love enough
to heal our wounds and grace
enough to see us through.

RABBITS, DOGS, HAWKS AND VULTURES

That darn rabbit persists within the backyard
despite our yellow lab that daily persists
in its retrieval, a quest for which he lives,
chasing it to the other side of the fence
where he can't go, where clover grows
the same, where bushes are better
for hiding, where no dogs roam.

The hawk, of course, cannot care less about
the fence, nor does he give a whit for the
dog, whose movements he has memorized.
It's fun to watch the dance as though we're
not involved, until the dog gains the angle
and breaks the rabbit's neck, and the vulture
beats the hawk to pick at its remains.

Most of the time, I am the rabbit, not so much
the dog, never the hawk. Vultures circle in the
skies nearby, occasionally swooping low to the
ground, so very vigilant. Just the other day as I
started walking, they perched in a line across
the peak of a neighbor's roof, while a hawk
flew overhead, all watching for one last misstep.

STINK BUG

I caught its movement out of the corner
of my eye while overhauling an old poem
in the middle of the night. Its slow
and measured stride spoke of purpose
and determination. With mounting curiosity,
I watched it trek across the pages of my work
until it stopped, as though to make a mental note,
no more impressed with what was written
than with my presence in its life. From where
in the poem my critic crawled I could not tell,
which left no better option than to plug
my nose, clear the desk, and start again.

"In my work, I really try to look at ordinary things quite closely to see if there isn't a little bit of something special about them."

—Ted Kooser

NOW LOOK WHAT YOU HAVE DONE, MR. KOOSER

I read your poem "Shame,"[ix] which shook me by surprise,
but not for what had shamed your subject, rueful as he is.
It is, ah ha, the sort of poem that I could write,
for all have hidden shame from which they cannot hide.

I grabbed my tablet, closed my eyes, and sent my happy
thoughts upstairs to rummage through the attic
and find me something I could use. What happened then
was stupefying – my thoughts repelled, sent

tumbling back down the stairs sprawling and dazed.
Their eyes refocused in time to see an oddly familiar shape
slam the attic door, nail it shut, steal the knob,
and disappear beneath the door as the attic light went out.

Though reeling, my persistent thoughts crawled to their feet,
determined to know what could have done such a thing.
Promptly, I flipped the page to read about the dancing fox
in the road and the joy you wished to share with me.[x]

SNOW

Two inches of climate change stopped by today,
stuck around, and decided to stay the night.
After all, it'd taken till mid-January to make
its way to this Mid-Atlantic state, plus all
the fuss and attention was fun to watch.
Back in Minnesota, no one seemed to care.
Here, three days ETA whipped up squalls
of newscast leads and breathless social media
posts. Two days out, the shelves were low
on bread and, *dear God help them*, toilet paper.

Then again, why not stay a few days,
check out jobs, like school bus driver
when schools reopen, or door-to-door snow
shovel salesman before the winter melts away,
or head of snowplow attachment for when
they get the truck started? How about political
speech writer for fixing blame on global warming,
or government drug pusher for frostbite vaccine
boosters? After all, it could take another year
to make it here again.

DRAIN

She called him late in the evening, long before cellphones and PCs, reaching him at the only phone on his dorm's third floor. Her sadness could not exceed his pride, because she called *him*, a bonified man of the cloth - to be. He'd mapped the course. Next stop, seminary.

Of course he would meet to talk. She was his friend, and so was Mike, his third-floor, Jones Hall dormmate. They'd come to him before, two as one in love, their wedding plans wedged between cocoons of discordant families – his Jewish, hers Catholic.

He jogged to her dorm's reception lounge where through the night they talked. It was Mike, their first real falling out, their parents stalking in the shadows, demanding this, that, and tearing their curtain of love. Mike had gone to walk it off, which was his quiet way.

She had as many questions as tears for what to do, all inflamed by fear their love would not survive. Lucky for her that *he* was there – *Mitigator, Commiserator, Counselor*. At nearly twenty, with accolades he wore like shiny studs on his lapel, he may as well have donned the collar.

At four in the morning, the quad was cold and still but for his quick, euphoric strides along the walkway to his dorm. His aspiration coat of many colors wrapped around his shoulders and fancied mitre stretched to fit his head provided all the warmth he needed.

So many years have passed and still he sees the puzzled looks as he enters his room and feels the blood and joy rushing from his face, his other friends in a circle on his dorm-room floor asking how he is, that awkward instance when you *think* you're talking about
the same thing....

"What's going on?"
"You don't know?"
"I've been with Sharon."
"We know – Mike's dead."

In the video loop still playing in his mind, he's sitting on
    the shower room floor,
water running, clothes soaked, and the memory of how he gets there
washed away. That isn't all the drain devours, like all that happened
after that until they walk the road to where Mike died. What is said along

the way, he still can't hear. He doubts it's more advice, or soothing words
of hope, or favorite passages. That he knows Mike's in Heaven, he still
can't say. That he takes her hand or she takes his for fear of what they face,
he can't recall. He sees the awful stain that marks the spot
    where they stop,

where Michael took his final breath. What thoughts and feelings
    they share
along the way are washed away. Over and over his mind
    just skips to packing
Michael's things – his pillow, socks, and favorite shirt; toothbrush, letters,
books, and everything that has his smell, that cries he's still alive.
    And then,

packing the car for Long Island – for a family he'd never met, for Michael's
burial – just a vague outline of the car the college let him take. Along
the way, it breaks down for lack of oil no one thought to check.
    Where it dies,
what town he's in, gone – down the drain. Just back and forth around

the car – a ghost-like movement's all he sees. No matter how hard
or many times he tries, he can't recall just how he repacks Michael's things,

or how he pays to ship them on ahead, or what becomes of the car,
    or who
he calls for help, if anyone at all. Where Sharon is and what becomes

of her, what happens to him after hitchhiking home – all is swept away.
The collar he never wears, the faces he cannot see, and voices
    he cannot hear
still clog the drain, building pressure strong enough to burst
    the aging pipe
from inside out, spilling all the moldy, rancid, poisonous gunk until there's
    nothing left but a stain on the road he walks alone.

FATHERS

They live to make their worldly dreams come true
for their children, from the moment of their birth,
the point at which the father's born, feeding from
      his umbilical sense of worth.

With every clamp and snip, as their children grow
and leave, they lunge for what is left of them,
dreams drowning in afterbirth, their sense
      of worth dripping from the surgeon's blade.

JUST VISITING

Having picked up the toys
and packed her things,
the car slowly backed to
the street, she and her Nana
waving. There was nothing
else to do but stand there
waving back, wondering why
his eyes would mist, his heart
would swell. Could it be
the thought that she was gone
again, or how she signaled
in their practiced way,
pointing to her eye,
crossing her arms to frame
her heart, and pointing back
to him again and again?

POETRY CONTEST

Einstein be damned, the clock is ticking!
Strapped in, the pressure's on,
pedal to metal and leaving tread
as I peel through my Random House,
faster, forward, beyond toward
the place I need to be –
I wonder who will win.

Circling, skidding, sliding, veering,
Googled roadkill left behind,
spinning, gunning past pages creased and scattered
through potholes *gaping* or *yawning*,
my windshield splattered with meter and rhyme
while Roget's heirs are jumping and cheering –
I wonder what my rivals do.

Fast upon a yellow wooded place
where the road becomes two diverging,
slowing, stopping, heart racing,
that way or the other and I can't take both!
("All the difference"[xi] one will make)
Revving the four-banger as if I knew,
I wonder where the others went.

Contender or creator idling there
with deadline ever looming,
wondering what a victory means,
two roads diverging from within –

Killing the engine, I jumped the fence
to where there are no judges waiting,
just "easy wind and downy flake."[xii]

MOM & DAD

I see you in the Kodak shot
    I use to mark the page,
which makes me wonder where you are
    while years here pass away.

The picture comes to life for me
    in ways the book will fail –
the clearing in the woods you loved
    where every chance you'd go

to hear the sounds of solitude
    and breathe in woodland balm.
It shows the wood you chopped and stacked
    for warmth and popping corn,

and through those trees a beaver dam
    you'd have to clear again.
A peaceful pose the two of you
    despite your guest's demand

to look for every photo op
    and freeze-frame memories.
The car is gone, the woodpile too,
    but not the same with you –

I see it in your countenance,
    two spirts passing through,
a visage of tranquility
    in sharing life anew.

Where you are I cannot know, except
   you're where you hoped to be,
where photos need not capture time,
   and love has set you free.

APOLLYON^{XIII}

He moves from bush
to bush, brushes past
my windowpanes,
and peeks inside to see
me hide. I pull the shades
and bolt the doors so not
to give him heed, but then
I hear him on the roof
and swear he's been
inside. The breach that
worries me the most –
a busted latch or broken
hinge or door left hanging
loose that helps the thief
in plundering my soul.

LAWN CHAIR

I don't know what happened to it, the folding kind
with fading blue nylon seat and back straps your dad
looped and crisscrossed side to side and front to back,

the one they'd fold and lean against the house out
back on the blacktop patio. It had a lightweight
frame that time and weather dulled.

We'd just come back from sitting with your dad,
not knowing he would soon be gone. Walking
toward the back door, your mom stopped to unfold

the chair and shake out the leaves. Even at the time,
it seemed like slow motion, except it happened fast,
the way she swung the chair above her head

beyond her tipping point and kept on falling back.
I froze in horror, but her grandson leapt from where
he stood on the steps and dove in time to catch

her head before it hit the patio. Her cries of
pain from broken bones still echo in my mind,
just as I relive us rushing back to City Hospital and sitting

by her side across the hall from where your father lay,
unaware and fighting for his life. Until these precious
two had passed and their home of sixty years had sold,

I didn't think about the chair. Till then it likely stayed
out back, leaning up against the house collecting leaves.
Today the house is there but not the chair, and where

it is I'd love to know. I'd drive as far as it would take
for just one chance to hoist it high above my head
and shake out leaves of retrospection. Then again,

it may be enough just driving by to see the thing's
no longer leaning against their home,
sniggering under its breath.

HAS YESTERDAY GONE?

Has yesterday gone, or is it dozing in an upstairs room,
or combing the basement to find its place among my things,
or sneaking through the kitchen spitting on the food I eat?
No doubt it wants my mobile phone and plans to work
my contact list to help make sure its footprint grows.

Don't tell me that it took my car and rushed to all
my navigation destinations, or wormed its way through all
my clothes to cling to me no matter where I go. Last night
I hoped when sleep took hold, there'd be relief at last, but
there it was in every dream – its faces, lies, and silent screams.

FOR BETTER OR FOR WORSE

By holding hands as we get old
you pull me from the dark and cold,
more looming, sometimes brooding,
often flirting, mesmerizing.

To feel your breath upon my chest
when close to you I'm finding rest
and hear your life's fragility,
its pulsing psalm sustaining me.

Your horror-ridden wails from depths
of sleep's strange consciousness
upon no gentler spirit ride
convincing me I must survive.

Our eyes, our ears, our breath entwined,
now fifty years our hearts aligned,
you've saved me from the dark and cold.
My gift to you? My demons' hold!

CULMINATION

I want to climb His highest peak
in hope my breath would mix
with Heaven's healing mist –

to rest upon the rocky brink with pine
that stretch from meagre soil
to sip the light of life –

to look below on mountain tops
I never dared to climb and lakes
I thought too deep to swim –

to reach from this world to the next
in hope that someone takes my hand,
and seraphs sing of love for one

repentant soul –
to feel the depths of darkness quake
and look into the eyes of God.

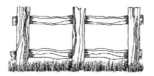

ABOUT THE AUTHOR

Chris Basher resides in Dover, Delaware with his wife, Sandy. He has published two other volumes of poetry: *Straining to Catch Every Leaf* (P.D. Kline, 2017) and *Spirit of the Adirondacks* (P.D. Kline, 2022). Also published is a "Mom's Choice Award" winning chapter book, *Finding Chloe* (P.D. Kline, 2023), and a number of essays. A middle grade novella, *Finding Friends*, is planned for release in 2024.

P. D. (Paul Donald) Kline, was the name given at birth. That name changed when he was adopted a couple of years later. Mr. Basher has worked in nonprofit, youth development services for more than 40 years. As an educator, he taught middle school and high school English, language arts, American literature, and creative writing.

For more information about Mr. Basher and his writing, visit www.pdklinebooks.com. He may be contacted at pdklinebooks@gmail.com.

ENDNOTES

i. Translated from La Campenella, 1851, by Franz Liszt. Regarded as one of the most difficult piano compositions to perform, requiring an astonishingly brisk allegretto tempo.

ii. The term is derived from the Greek province of the same name which dates to antiquity; the province's mountainous topography and sparse population of pastoralists later caused the word *Arcadia* to develop into a poetic byword for an idyllic vision of unspoiled wilderness. Arcadia is a poetic term associated with bountiful natural splendor and harmony.

iii. Scott, T, Director. 2004. "Man On Fire." 20th Century Fox. (Lupita "Pita" Ramos)

iv. Ibid

v. Romans 12:21

vi. Iron Maiden - A notorious medieval torture device that consisted of a human-sized box with spikes on the inside.

vii. Brazen Bull - A brutal torture and execution device, perhaps history's worst, allegedly used in ancient Greece.

viii. Pear of Anguish - A particularly cruel medieval torture device. Its various uses included insertion into a person's mouth and the torturer turning a screw mechanism to expand the device and cause excruciating pain.

ix. Kooser, Ted. 2020. *Red Stilts.* "Shame," p. 75. Copper Canyon Press.

x. Kooser, Ted. 2020. *Red Stilts*, "Driving to Dwight," p. 77. Copper Canyon Press.

xi. Robert Frost, "The Road Not Taken" (*Mountain Interval*, New York: Henry Holt and Company, 1916)

xii. Robert Frost, "Stopping by Woods on a Snowy Evening" (*New Hampshire*, 1923)

xiii. *Revelation* 9:11.